Praise fo

Upside Down is a testament to what love and faith in God has done, can do and continues to do. This book is the true story of the blessing that is Kyle, and how she touches the lives of everyone around her. One of my favorite Dale Archer sayings is, "When you are always trying to conform to the norm, you lose your uniqueness, which can be the foundation for your greatness." This book about Kyle and her family made me laugh, made me cry, and made me thankful I am fortunate enough to have met them.

Pam Hunsaker, Regional Director, Dolly Parton Imagination Library

In my opinion, Marv Loucks has a passion for and a belief in the ability of individuals to change their lives through hard work, study, association with people of faith, and seeking out positive mentors. He continues to devote his time and talent to help individuals and families face life's challenges, grow and prosper for the greater good. Use Upside Down as a tool to help mold your understanding of real life circumstances and the strength to face challenges.

George Lawson, President, Knox Electronics

Working beside Marv professionally and personally for the past 17 years, I have come to the conclusion that if anyone can turn upside down into right side up regardless of the circumstances or magnitude of the challenges, it is Marv Loucks. He has such an unwavering conviction to make his corner of the world a better place. The fruits of his work are real and plentiful and this book is but one example of how he continually shares his wisdom and life's lessons learned so selflessly with all who have the privilege of spending time with him in any capacity.

Dr. Jacqueline Vietti, President Emeritus, Butler Community College

The book, Upside Down, is a wonderful depiction of life. All of God's people will face challenges, He clearly tells us in the Bible to expect to be tested; however, in order to persevere through challenging times, we must remain thankful, regardless. I have known Kyle for many years, and I can honestly say, every time I am around her, even if it's brief, I see Jesus...her huge heart and sincere love for people, makes her truly unique.

I have often wondered why children are born with special needs, and why families have to experience the challenges associated with special needs children, and after reading Upside Down, it is clear, Kyle's family wouldn't have her any other way, she is no different. God loves Kyle and He knows the impact her life will have on those she meets. Kyle's legacy will include people just like me who have been touched by Kyle's love that knows no boundaries, her inspiring sweet spirit, and her ability to use a hug and a smile to positively impact the people around her.

Kyle's Dad, thank you for writing this book, for sharing your honest feelings, but more importantly for allowing your heart to be displayed on each page.

Rich Morris, VP Strategic Partnerships, Acumen Brands

Upside Down

Marv Loucks

Published by
Innovo Publishing LLC
www.innovopublishing.com
1-888-546-2111

Providing Full-Service Publishing Services for
Christian Authors, Artists & Organizations: Hardbacks, Paperbacks,
eBooks, Audiobooks, Music & Film

UPSIDE DOWN
Copyright © 2014 by Marv Loucks
All rights reserved.

ISBN 13: 978-1-61314-194-6

Cover Design & Interior Layout: Innovo Publishing LLC

Printed in the United States of America
U.S. Printing History

First Edition: February 2014

Dedicated to Kerri and Kyle.
I love you and thank God for you.

Table of Contents

Foreword

The American novelist, essayist, playwright, and poet James Baldwin stated, "Not everything that is faced can be changed. But nothing can be changed until it is faced" (ThinkExist). This statement rings clear and true when I reflect on the life lessons, attitude adjustments, inspiration gained, and friendships built as I have been afforded the opportunity to be connected with Marv, Kerri, and Kyle Loucks, and the extended Boyer-Martin-Loucks families.

Having relocated my family to the El Dorado, Kansas, area during the mid-1970s, I was aware of Marv's presence in the community through his radio work around local sportscasts and his officiating. Later upon his marriage to one of the "Martin" daughters, the connection within our church fellowship allowed me to begin a new and growing awareness of Marv's talents, leadership, and passion for family, church, community, and education, especially after the birth of Kyle and the need to face life-altering issues.

Kyle's birth and subsequent major medical needs brought our church family together in prayer, support, and growth as a Body of Believers in God's power to face challenges and change lives. The Boyer-Martin-Loucks families not only faced the challenges, but provided examples and leadership to the community at large. I have been blessed to have been a benefactor of these growth experiences, as my family has faced dissimilar, but serious challenges, with children and grandchildren.

In my opinion, Marv Loucks has a passion for and a belief in the ability of individuals to change their lives through hard work, study, association with people of faith, and seeking out positive mentors. He continues to devote his time and talent to help individuals and families face life's challenges, grow, and prosper for the greater good. Use *Upside Down* as a tool to help mold your understanding of real-life circumstances and the strength to face challenges.

George Lawson,
Friend

Preface

I had the idea for this book twenty-three years ago, shortly after our daughter, Kyle, was born. I wanted to write a book about her—about us. I even had a title. But I did not have the confidence to write it. When I found the confidence, I did not have the self-discipline. Now, as I look back, I could never have written the book then because I really did not have one. It was still being written.

Upside Down is the story of how a girl with Down syndrome changed a man, a family, and a community. I am not sure who or where I would be if God had not intervened and brought Kyle into our lives. I am sure beyond any doubt that I would not be the man I am today.

My first thought when writing this book was to simply introduce you to Kyle and share a little about Down syndrome. As I began writing, my focus changed. The real message is this: you will face adversity in life, and you can overcome it. Author and speaker Jon Gordon said, "Adversity is not a dead-end but a detour to a better outcome" (Gordon).

I read every day. My bookshelves are full of books written by authors like Jon Gordon, Zig Ziglar, Pat Williams, John Maxwell, and others who teach, challenge, and inspire. I do not want to suggest for one minute that this is such a book. However, I do hope that my family's experience will encourage you to reflect more, reach higher, grow in your faith, love more unconditionally, give more freely, live more fully, and persevere more intently as you endure life's trials.

Your life is not over. You are still writing your own legacy. Do not get to the end of your life and have regret. Finish strong.

Chapter 1

Who Is This Girl Who Changed My Life?

Chick-Fil-A recorded a video blog a few years ago, entitled *Every Life Has a Story*. You can view it on the company's website. It showed several people in one of their restaurants—customers and employees—going about their daily lives. There was a caption with each face. A man who had just received the news that he was cancer-free; the lady who had just lost her husband of forty-nine years; a young girl who had lost her mother, and a dad who blamed her; a teenage boy abandoned by his parents; and a dad whose son had recently been deployed. Each person had a life story. All of us have a story. I am sharing mine in hopes that you will find encouragement.

If that video had shown Kyle, the caption might have read, "This twenty-three-year-old spends several hours per week serving kindergarten students and senior citizens."

When Kyle was born, my wife, Kerri, and I, knew nothing about Down syndrome or that some children would be higher functioning than others. When we learned that there were degrees of severity, we prayed that Kyle would be in the percentile of higher-functioning kids, and we lived as if that was going to be the case. Our family is blessed that Kyle is high functioning. Part of that, we believe, is just who she is. And part of it might be the fact that our support structure was extremely strong.

Within minutes after bringing Kyle home from the hospital, Kerri's sisters told her, "You will not be overprotective." We have instilled discipline, but we also allowed Kyle to be a kid and have a life that is as normal as possible. She attended school with her peers, experienced numerous summer camps, and played the piano. Currently, she sings in the adult church choir, volunteers every week, and competes in multiple sports.

Here are some words that best describe Kyle:

Outgoing
Energetic
Cute
Charming
Funny
Grateful
Determined
Forgiving
Tolerant
A friend
Prayerful
Spiritual

I have never seen a child with as much pain tolerance as my daughter. She is tough. I did not witness this, but Kerri did. Kyle participates in the Special Olympics in several sports. One evening during her final season, she was hit in the mouth by a line drive. I was at a meeting that evening and did not attend, but I was told it sounded as bad as it looked. After the bleeding stopped and with lips three times their normal size, she asked, "When is it my turn to bat?" Other parents watching with Kerri were astonished by Kyle's toughness. She no longer plays softball.

She is also sensitive. During a race at practice one afternoon, she was ahead of the other runners when she suddenly stopped. We asked her later why she stopped running in the middle of the race. She told us she was waiting on the others to catch up.

Then there is her memory, the likes of which, I am not sure I have seen before. It is a steel trap. Do not try to slip something past her. The girl does not forget a thing. I am still amazed at the way she can recall exactly where she was when she heard a particular song. Do not even challenge her to a game of *Name that Tune* if the topic is country music. You will lose. Upon hearing as few as two or three notes, she can tell you the artist and song title.

She loves singing in our church choir, which is apparent on Sunday mornings. She sings every song with all of her heart, and rarely looks at her music.

Her outgoing spirit is a sight to see at the grocery store. She knows so many people and wants to visit with all of them. She doesn't just know people; she knows about them. After five minutes with them, she will tell you what they had for lunch, the names of their children, and their ages. This is how it is when she delivers Meals on Wheels to about a half dozen people every Wednesday. She knows about Dick, Mary, Roy, Billie, and Wanda. Dick and Mary prefer juice; Roy wants skim milk; and Wanda requests 2% milk.

Kyle would rather watch people than assist us with grocery shopping. She prefers the bench in the lobby of Wal-Mart because of the accessibility to a greater number of people. Then, on the way home, she delivers a report about the people who had been shopping, what they purchased, and what they will

15

have for dinner. She will also often ask about their faith and how their life is on that particular day.

I cannot tell you how many lives she has touched. Countless. It led me to write a song.

Countless Lives

I could not wait to hold you when you came into this world,
I really didn't care if you were a boy or a girl.
You were a precious gift from God, loved by your family.
We loved those little things that others could not see.

Chorus

Countless lives, countless lives, you've touch countless lives in
*   many ways,*
We know that others see the Lord in you today.
Countless lives, countless lives, you've touched countless lives, you've
*   touched countless lives.*

The doctor knew that something was wrong,
What'er it was, we would be strong (we'd be strong);
Your fragile heart was formed by God's hand,
And we gave you up into God's plan (into God's plan).

Chorus

You taught us about love and taught us very well (oh so well),
With your mended heart, our miracle.
Once there was no hope for kids like you,
But time has shown the truth.
You've touched so many lives, our miracle come true.

Chorus

One of the lives she touched was her friend Megan. Megan is our pastor's daughter. She was seven when her family moved to our community. She did not want to move when her father was called to serve as our senior pastor. Megan is in college now. As she looks back, she says she realizes that had her family not moved to our community, she would never have met Kyle, and if she had never met Kyle, she might not have decided to study music therapy.

We were praying one night with some friends at our church. Kyle is a bold prayer. Part of her prayer was, "Dear God, thank You for my dad. He changed my life." That was sweet and so thoughtful of her. But the truth is she is the one who has changed lives, beginning with mine. I see life differently than I did before she was born. She has made me a better person.

She loves people and she wants to make sure they know God in a personal way. It was a beautiful thing to see one of Kyle's friends get baptized on Easter Sunday. Her decision to be baptized was due, in part, to Kyle's encouragement.

Since Kyle's baptism at age ten, she continues to be captivated by this experience; she still gets excited about it. In fact, if you so much as dip your toes in a swimming pool, she will move beside you, grab your arm, and pronounce, "I baptize you in the name of the Father, the Son, and the Holy Spirit."

Chapter 2

Adversity

In the days following the attacks on September 11, Billy Graham spoke at a church service at Washington's National Cathedral. Rev. Graham remarked, "It is said that adversity introduces us to ourselves." That is certainly true in my life. I have experienced my fair share. God has used each experience to make me stronger.

In his book, *The 15 Invaluable Laws of Growth*, John Maxwell devoted an entire chapter to the Law of Pain. Maxwell wrote, "I have never known anyone who said, 'I love problems,' but I have known many who have admitted that their greatest gains came in the middle of the pain" (Maxwell, 2012, 124). You can count me among that group. Maxwell said the painful experiences in his life have taught him to let the discomfort be a catalyst for development.

That has to be your mindset. Take this motto of the US Navy Seals as your own. "I will never quit. I persevere and thrive on adversity. If I get knocked down, I will get back up, every time."

Chris and Kerry Shook, who founded The Fellowship of the Woodlands in Houston, Texas, wrote a book entitled, *One Month to Live*. In it they write, "At no other point in life is the substance of our character refined more than when we are facing what seems to be insurmountable odds or overwhelming situations. When we understand that struggles and difficulties represent opportunities for growth in our lives, then we will respond to them with an entirely new motivation" (Shook, 2008).

Down syndrome and medical issues overwhelmed us. We simply prayed and forged ahead, one day at a time, or even a few hours at a time. On days when we could not pray, others interceded for us.

I believe God does not bring problems, but He allows them. Trials and hardships make us stronger. We must endure them. My friend, Dick Gorham, wrote a book entitled, *It's Just Life: A Small Story Within a Greater Story*. He wrote, "Blessings often come in unexpected ways and in difficult circumstances" (Gorham, 2009, 113). Down syndrome was unexpected and, at times, difficult. Yet every day there has been a blessing. Kyle has taught us a new dimension of love.

The list of people who have dealt with extraordinary adversity is endless. Those who have persevered are stronger for it. Here are just a few examples.

Adversity made my friend's college roommate stronger. She was one of eleven children. Their mother died, and they were facing life with an alcoholic father. Many nights he came home and passed out. He was worse than a nonfactor. He was a detriment. She was determined to have a better life, and that motivated her to earn a college degree.

Dr. Jan Brunstrom became a doctor. She also has cerebral palsy. She said all her life people told her what she could not do. If she would have listened to the naysayers, she would not have walked, graduated as valedictorian at age sixteen, and most certainly would not have become a pediatric neurologist. She used to tell the kids who came to her clinic that it is not fair for them to have CP, but that they had two choices: they could crawl into a corner until they died, or they could fight back. Choose to fight.

Loretta Claiborne is a distance runner. She has competed in more than twenty-five marathons, finishing twice in the top 100 at the Boston marathon. Doctors had predicted she would never walk and encouraged her mother to put her in an institution. She was born legally blind and mentally retarded. At age four, she received an operation that restored her sight, and later she earned her college degree.

CJ Johnson is a young man who served as a counselor at Heather's Camp, a camp in the Midwest for young people who are blind or have low vision. CJ is nearly blind himself. But he did not allow his lack of sight to steal his vision. CJ is a certified lifeguard, a certified lifeguard trainer, and an EMT. When I last spoke to him, he was studying to be a paramedic. Do not miss CJ's message. He told a group of us, "The world is not going to adapt to me, so I have to adapt to the world."

When you face adversity, the world will not temporarily stop and make adjustments for you. Harvard psychologist William James wrote that the greatest discovery of his generation is that a human can alter his life by altering his attitude. Best-selling author and speaker Harvey Mackay added that it might not be our fault for being down, but it is our fault for not getting up. The late Zig Ziglar said, "You don't drown by falling in water, you drown by staying there" (Ziglar, 1990, 12).

Life is like golf. There will be hazards in our path and not all of our shots will be good. Golf professional Bob Duvall offered good advice when he said not to dwell on what just happened, whether it was great or terrible; just move on and play the next shot.

So, let me encourage you to work through your trials. Don't worry or act out of fear. Max Lucado says that worry is an option, not an assignment.

Chapter 3

What Down Syndrome Has Taught Me

Having a child with Down syndrome is the last thing we ever expected. However, it was the best thing that has happened to us. Kyle's birth was a defining moment in our marriage and our lives.

Life with Kyle has been a blessing, but it has not been without some adversity and a few anxious moments. Our family—immediate and extended—is better and stronger because of the challenges we have faced. Our faith and our marriage have been tested and strengthened. We have had to summon the courage to change the things we could change, and we have learned to be content with that which we cannot change.

I unintentionally and regrettably heaped added stress on Kerri when Kyle was younger. I did not want Kyle to believe that Down syndrome was an excuse for misbehavior. When Kyle did not immediately follow directions, I became impatient. I lost my patience much too often. That led to numerous arguments. Kerri said, at times, it would have been easier for her to have just walked away. She didn't, and we did agree that Kyle needed discipline, but I could not expect her to immediately do what I was asking. She needed more time to process it.

Looking back on Kyle's life, I regret the hurt I caused Kerri and the uneasiness I brought upon my family because of my impatience and unrealistic demands on Kyle. I had to change, but I will never regret trying to instill discipline in her life. We have seen too many children, both those with special needs and the stereotypical normal kids, who could have benefited from more discipline when they were younger.

Living in a world with Down syndrome has taught me several things. First, you can do more than you think you can. Running away was certainly not an option. It was never even a consideration. Never! I had no idea what our lives would be like. I was clueless as to what to do or where to start as a dad. I knew it would not be easy, but because of our faith in God, I knew we would be all right. One thing that made it easier was the support of our families. In other words, we had as much support as new parents could ask for.

Second, there are some really special people in the world who want to walk beside you. We have had no shortage of special people in our lives.

When Kyle was born, many people told us that God only gives kids with Down syndrome to special people. I graciously thanked them for trying to comfort us, but frankly, there were several days when I did not feel very special.

Throughout Kyle's life, we have learned who the truly special people are. They are the teachers, therapists, camp counselors, Sunday school teachers, Special Olympics coaches, Young Life leaders, and others. They are the special ones because they have given much, and selflessly, so Kyle would have a normal life experience.

In addition to our families, who have given us so much, and so selflessly, there have been countless friends.

There is one special family whose support cannot possibly be measured. They are as close as our own family.

Dave and Judy Slayton, and their daughter, Paige, literally treat Kyle as if she was their biological child. Kyle even jokes that they are her real parents and that we are her "rental parents."

Judy was Kyle's second-grade teacher. Today, she has Kyle help in her classroom one day a week. Paige, although she is two years younger than Kyle, is a big sister to her. They are inseparable, and they fight over the front seat (shotgun!).

Our families are close. Life is easier when you have strong friendships. I would not want to go through life without the Slayton family.

Miss Glenda has been invaluable to me in her service on various committees. She helps Kyle live more independently. Kyle cannot drive, in large part to her poor vision, so Glenda, who also sings in the choir, gives Kyle a ride to church every Sunday. That allows Kyle to go somewhere without her parents having to take her.

Miss Phyllis, a grandmotherly type who has a heart for young kids, walked closely with Kyle when she was very young. Phyllis was a Sunday school helper at church. Because of Phyllis, we knew Kyle would be well taken care of at church when we were not with her.

Jane Constance, who was Kyle's speech therapist, and Donna Neal, her physical therapist also played key parts in Kyle's life. Early intervention is critical for any child, especially one with special needs. Good therapists help identify individual strengths and weaknesses. Jane only worked with a few private clients. When we first learned about her, we were not sure she would accept Kyle as a client. She later told us she liked that we were devoted parents, and we seemed like a good match. She also had a strong message for us: take care of our marriage. She told us that nearly 75 percent of parents of a child with special needs would divorce. She did not want us to be a statistic.

We believe what she did for Kyle was immeasurable. Children with Down syndrome have low tongue tone. Speech therapy helped with oral motor/feeding, which is the foundation for oral speech, development of oral speech, and receptive and expressive language.

If you are a parent or know parents of a newborn with Down syndrome, strongly encourage them to seek a meeting with speech and physical therapists.

Amanda, Kyle's Young Life leader, said, "One of my favorite Kyle moments was the first day I met her. It was my first day, and I was being introduced to the Young Life committee and their families. Kyle comes up to me as I am sitting down. She walks up real close, puts her hand on my head, and ruffles my hair all up. Kerri was mortified because Kyle knows how to 'be polite,' but it was that moment that made me comfortable. Kyle broke down my boundaries without even trying. She shares her genuine self and welcomes all into her world as she reflects a special relationship with Christ. Kyle is an angel with many questions and a heart of gold."

Third, I have been reminded, almost daily, of my need to depend on God more. I will never forget the day I heard God speak to me in as distinct a voice as I have ever heard. Nothing He has spoken to me through His Holy Spirit since then has been clearer. Early one morning while on my way to a train station to pick up a friend, I received this unmistakable message: "Marv, I gave you Kyle, and I created people like her so people like you would depend on me more." I was driving at the time, so I pulled over to the side of the road to write it down.

In this life, you get increasing strength by going from struggle to struggle. We have had our share of struggles. We are stronger because of them. Abraham Lincoln said, "The struggle of today, is not altogether for today—it is for a vast future also."

Chapter 4

Miracles Do Happen

I used to wonder if miracles really happen. I do not have to wonder anymore. I have experienced some.

The first miracle came about seven hours after Kyle was born. Kerri called me from her hospital bed at about two in the morning to tell me the doctor wanted to talk to me. His message was the last thing I ever thought I would hear: he suspected that our daughter had Down syndrome.

For many years before Kyle was born, seeing an individual with a mental or physical impairment bothered me to such an extent that I purposely moved away to avoid seeing them. I could not handle seeing them, whatever their disability. I felt guilty that I was so healthy and they were not.

That phone call in the middle of the night changed my life. Running away was never an option. There was no place to run to except to God. But I had to have strength, and I needed to find it quickly.

I found the strength I needed in my faith. I remember speaking to a men's group about two months before Kyle was born. I do not know what prompted me to talk about people with special needs, but I do remember, like it was yesterday, telling them that even if our baby was born with health problems, I would be able to deal with it. I was certain I would not have to worry about that because I believed God knew how sensitive and emotional I became when I was around them. It just would not happen, until and unless God changed my heart. It happened, and He changed my heart.

On the night Kyle was born, I called my mother-in-law. I learned later that she was not surprised by the news because of a dream and newspaper article—she shared the following:

It was October or November 1990 that I woke up from a dream that left me shaken. I don't usually remember any dreams I have, but this one really bothered me because it was about a woman having a baby that had something wrong with it. It soon became apparent that the baby had Down syndrome. Since Kerri was expecting a baby in January, it was particularly upsetting. Soon after that dream, there was an article in the newspaper written by the aunt of a Down syndrome baby who had been put in an institution because his parents did not want him and the trouble he would cause them the rest of his life. The aunt was just horrified to think that the parents were so uncaring and felt no love for their child, and she even considered taking him to raise herself. I began thinking how I would react if that were my grandchild, and I really was not certain I could handle such a situation. I did not say anything about my dream to anyone, but when Marv called me early on the morning of February 1 and said there was something wrong with our baby, I knew immediately what it was, although he kept saying there was something wrong with her heart. All day long people called and prayed. Doctors and nurses kept assuring us she would be all right if we could get her to Wichita, but that was not possible because a winter storm had moved in. The only way to get her there was to by air. She earned her wings at the age of one day. I kept thinking of the article I had read, and I knew there was no way we would not want to take her home and love and care for her.

When Kyle was about three years old, the lady who had written the article came to meet her. She told us her nephew had died. I would imagine he died because he did not have a loving family and community surrounding him as Kyle did.

The Miracle at Mayo

One common characteristic of children with Down syndrome is Atrioventricular (AV) Canal Defect. Kyle was born with AV Canal, which is a combination of several abnormalities of the heart present at birth. The defect occurs when there is a hole between the chambers of the heart, and there are problems with the valves that regulate blood flow in the heart. The AV Canal allows extra blood to circulate to the lungs. Ensuing problems overwork the heart and cause it to enlarge.

Her heart defect eventually required surgery, which she received at the Mayo Clinic in Rochester, Minnesota, in June 1991. Our family expected to be in Minnesota for about two weeks following Kyle's surgery. We were there two months. Her heart surgery was successful, but she developed a virus that nearly took her life. At one point, her team of doctors told us they had done all they could to save her. That day, June 30, 1991, was perhaps the darkest day of my life.

I returned home for a few days to work. I had planned to return to Rochester to be with Kyle, Kerri, and the rest of our family who had been by our side during the extended hospital stay. On the day I planned to return to Rochester, Kerri called and said to hurry, that I needed to get there as soon as I could. Kyle's condition was deteriorating quickly.

With the help of several friends, I was able to find a private pilot who would fly me back to Minnesota. On the plane, I began visiting with the pilot. I learned he and his wife had recently lost their seventeen-month-old son. He was Kyle's age. I truly believed that God was preparing me for the loss of our daughter.

If losing Kyle before her second birthday was God's plan for us, we would have accepted it. We had no regrets for electing to have surgery. Without it, doctors told us Kyle's life expectancy would likely be about twenty years. That wasn't good enough. We could not stand the thought of watching her slowly die right in front of our eyes in our home. We had to give her a chance at life. To do otherwise, I believe, would have been irresponsible.

Kerri's mom was at the airport when we landed. She was the first person I saw when I stepped off the plane. I remember asking her if Kyle was still alive, all but sure that I knew the answer. She was still alive and improving significantly.

One of her doctors at the Mayo Clinic said there were not many people as tough as little girls with Down syndrome. I believe that is true. I know Kyle is one tough young lady.

Finally, on July 27, 1991, fifty-five days after entering the hospital, Kyle was dismissed and we brought her home.

There was one more test. In the first few nights after we brought her home, there were sleepless nights for all of us. Several times, we strolled with Kyle around our neighborhood after midnight trying to make her comfortable. We believed she was experiencing withdrawal from two months of heavy medication she received during her hospitalization. Thankfully, that subsided after a few weeks.

The Empty Parking Lot

There was one more night when I believe God placed a hedge of protection around Kyle.

One evening she attended a concert with a small group of friends. There was an adult chaperone with the kids, but he was assisting a couple of them who were in wheelchairs. The concert was on the campus of a large university. As they were leaving, Kyle did not notice that the rest of her group went one direction while she veered the other way; she followed the crowd exiting the arena doors. She continued walking and eventually found herself on the outskirts of the campus in an empty parking lot. Kyle was unfamiliar with the area, and her vision was brutally poor. It was a rainy night, and she did not have her cell phone or identification with her. That was an opportunity for disaster.

She stood alone in the dark, lonely parking lot. There was only one vehicle in the lot, and it was leaving. Suddenly, it stopped and the back door opened. The occupant had caught her purse strap in the door. The young lady happened to see Kyle and told the driver to wait. The lady was Kyle's cousin, Danae, and the driver was her aunt Karla, Kerri's sister.

God and I had a long conversation later that night, and I did most of the talking. I was thanking Him for saving my eighteen-year-old daughter from potential harm.

Chapter 5

Funny Girl

Kyle was looking at pictures with Kerri one day and saw one of herself. She asked, "Mom, how old was I then?" Kerri answered that she was probably about four. Kyle replied, "Wow, I really had Down syndrome that day."

Speaking to a classroom of third-grade students, she was asked what Down syndrome was. She replied, "It means I have fun."

Kyle has always been fascinated with Down syndrome and what it means. We explained to her that she has an extra chromosome. One day she came to Kerri with a troubled look on her face. Kerri asked if she was okay. Kyle told her that her extra chromosome was hurting. Kerri asked her to point to where it hurt. When Kyle pointed to her lower stomach, Kerri realized she was cramping; she had started her period.

During her annual physical, Kyle looked around the small examining room at Kerri and the doctor and asked, "Are we all girls here?" Being assured that they were all girls, Kyle proceeded to ask the doctor to "explain mammogram stuff."

We were traveling in Wisconsin one time and Kerri asked, "Kyle, what is the capital of Wisconsin?" Kyle calmly stated, "The W."

Kyle and her case manager were discussing Kyle's future in general. Her case manager asked, "Kyle, how do you see yourself in five years?" Kyle replied, "In the mirror."

Before she could spell very well, I would spell words to Kerri very fast so Kyle would not have time to figure out what I was saying. That apparently irritated Kyle. In her frustration, she yelled, "Mom, Dad is spelling in cursive."

On another occasion, Kyle pushed her mother a little too far and Kerri grounded her. Later, Kyle asked Kerri, "Mom, how can you ground a Down syndrome child?"

One day, Kerri told her that she was lucky because she had her dad's legs. Kyle was not amused. In fact, it drove her to tears, through which she blurted, "I want my own legs."

Every time we go to Starbucks, Kyle orders water. It is automatic and it does not cost $4 per cup. The baristas always abbreviate the order with a permanent marker on the side of the cup. On this particular day, Kyle finally lost her patience. "They did it again," she angrily proclaimed. "Who did what?" we asked. "That lady." Clueless about the barista's offense, we asked what it was that had Kyle so agitated. "She wrote H Twenty on my cup." (H_2O for water)

Our family tries to eat healthy. Kerri is more successful than Kyle and I. The two of us do not always adhere to the healthy menu. We often push the limit. One evening when Kerri asked Kyle what she wanted for dinner, she replied, "Mom, how about something processed?"

One Saturday morning Kerri and I were sitting in the kitchen visiting over coffee. Kyle was in her room at the other end of our house. Out of nowhere, came a voice. It was Kyle, saying to whoever was on the phone with her, "I want a beef, a pepperoni, and here is my dad." Kyle handed me the phone, and

I learned that it was a local pizzeria. Kyle had ordered pizza about two hours before lunch. The young lady understood and graciously cancelled our order. We were not mad. We were surprised but thrilled that she knew her way around a telephone book and could successfully complete the transaction.

I was teasing Kyle mercilessly one morning. She had finally had enough and said, "You're a pain in the butt." She then asked Kerri, "Am I old enough to say that?"

She could also stop you in your tracks with things that were not so funny. When we travel on business, Kyle usually stays with her grandmother. In one conversation at Grandma's house, Kyle told her, "Grandma, I am tired of having Down syndrome. I want to be a normal person."

Sorry, kid. God knew exactly what He was doing when He created you. He said as much in Psalm 139:13–14: "For you created my inmost being; you knit me together in my mother's womb. I praise you because I am fearfully and wonderfully made."

Chapter 6

Don't Quit

Do not believe for one minute that you will go through life without trials and adversity. That is a fantasy world. When you face difficulty or misfortune, don't quit. Here are three reasons not to quit when adversity interrupts your life. I learned these lessons early in life, and they have helped me as a dad.

First, adversity is inevitable. You WILL face adversity sometime in your life. You probably already have. Maybe you are right now. You have to have a plan and options to deal with it. "Consider it pure joy, my brothers, whenever you face trials of many kinds, because you know the testing of your faith develops perseverance. Perseverance must finish its work so that you may be mature and complete, not lacking anything" (James 1:2–4). If you are a parent, you will surely experience much joy. But challenges are inevitable.

Second, adversity will be inconvenient. There will not likely be a warning track alerting you that you are very close to the outfield wall or rumble strips like you drive over as you approach a stop sign on a busy highway. You might be going through life thinking everything is great. Then BAM! Adversity does not keep regular office hours. It might pound on your door unannounced at 3:00 a.m. Or it might barge right in without even knocking. Be ready. As the late Zig Ziglar once said, "You cannot tailor make the situations in life, but you can tailor make the attitudes to fit this situations before they arise" (Ziglar, 1990, 4).

Sometimes kids get sick in the middle of the night. Sometimes, like Kyle, they need to be hospitalized. We expected her to be in the hospital for two weeks. It ended up being two *months*. The hospital was more than five hundred miles from home. Inconvenient? Yes, but that hospital in Minnesota was exactly where we were supposed to be.

Finally, your trials will be invaluable, if you learn how to respond to them. Often I have reacted to situations when I wish I had responded. There is a difference. "And the God of all grace, who called you to his eternal glory, after you have suffered a little while, will himself restore you and make you strong, firm and steadfast" (1 Peter 5:10).

Having a child with Down syndrome and a heart defect was invaluable. Had that not happened, I would not be the person I am today. Life can beat you up. Don't let it get you down or keep you down. Adversity will make you better or bitter. You have to decide.

There is a story I like to read in the second chapter of the gospel of Mark (2:1–6). It is the story of Jesus healing a paralytic. Jesus was at a home in Capernaum, his adopted hometown. So many people were gathered that there was no room left, not even outside the front door. While Jesus was preaching, some men came to the home. Four men were carrying a paralytic to see Jesus. They could not get to Jesus because a large crowd had gathered. So they made an opening in the roof of the house. They removed some tiles from the roof and lowered the mat the paralyzed man was lying on. When Jesus saw their faith, He said to the paralytic, "Son, your sins are forgiven." I do not know anything about the affliction of the man who was brought to

Jesus. One might assume it was serious because his four friends were desperate to get him to Jesus quickly. They were persistent and creative. They took drastic measures and fought for their friend. Whether you are a parent or not, I hope you have friends who will fight for you in your time of need.

No one ever had to carry Kyle on a mat and lower her through a rooftop, but many people walked beside her. They prayed for her on her worst days, loved her unconditionally, and gave her opportunities. There were people we will never know about who were persistent in interceding for her.

The four friends of the paralytic man in Mark's gospel did not quit until they succeeded in getting him to Jesus. Sometimes quitting is easier than persevering. I am glad I did not quit on my family. Quitting would have been irresponsible, and I would have missed many blessings.

I have to admit that quitting did cross my mind for a moment while vacationing one summer in Colorado. I was climbing Mt. Chrysolite. The elevation is 12,822 feet and the final few feet were brutal. It took everything I had plus the encouragement of my friends to finish. Once I finished, I found the view to be splendid.

Looking back, there was never really any question; I had to finish that climb. I could not allow myself to get that close to the top of the mountain and not finish. It would have been a wasted effort, and I would have had to live with the regret the rest of my life.

I have seen and experienced too much in my life to quit easily. I have seen it in sports, in business, in marriages, and in hospitals. I watched God use a team of doctors and nurses to save Kyle's life *after* they said they could do nothing more to save her.

What are you dealing with today? Keep battling through your challenges. Don't stop short of the mountaintop. You do not want to miss the blessings. More importantly, you do not want to carry the regret with you the rest of your life.

I found a card I had written to Kyle while she was at the Mayo Clinic. Her grandpa hand delivered it to her June 30, 1991, the day doctors told our family there was nothing more they could do. I wrote, "Keep fighting. Don't give up. We will win." Someone must have read it to her, and she must have been listening.

Bill Wedekind served with the First Marine Division, First Reconnaissance Battalion, near Da Nang, Vietnam, before encountering a booby trap. It left him without sight and without his hands. For the next eighteen months, Wedekind lay in a hospital. "Quitting was never a possibility," he said. When he returned home, his grandmother thought he could become a successful potter. He did. His work is beautiful. A headline above a framed article I have about Wedekind reads, "No Sight, No Hands, No Will to Quit."

Tammy Duckworth could have quit and given up on life, but she did not. Ms. Duckworth was elected to Congress in 2012, six years after losing in her first bid for the US House of Representatives. She walks the halls of Congress on prosthetic limbs. Representative Duckworth served in the Iraq War as a helicopter pilot. She lost both legs in a 2004 grenade attack. Ms. Duckworth has championed the rights of people with disabilities since returning from the Iraq War, where she said she could have been left for dead. She refers to this current time in her life as "bonus time."

If you think about it, we are all living on bonus time. We do not know when life will end. At a basketball game, you can see the clock and the seconds ticking away. Eventually the game will end. We are living our lives without the benefit of a game clock. None of us is guaranteed a long life. I could die before you finish this book or live another twenty-five years. The key is not to waste any heartbeats.

Your will to win must be stronger than the struggles you are facing. I recall a saying from Simon T. Bailey: losers look at what they are going through. Champions look at what they are going to.

Do not miss this point. I am in no way insinuating that you are a loser. But many good people have given entirely too much thought as to what they are going *through* when, in fact, their real effort and energy should be on their ultimate goal—what they are going *to*. They simply lose their focus.

In life, remember these things:

Fight for your friends.
Focus on today.
Do not quit.

They will serve you well.

Chapter 7

No Excuses

In his book, *Better Than Good*, Zig Ziglar included a story about a young man named Kyle Maynard. Kyle was a champion wrestler in high school. He was good enough to wrestle in college. Oh, and by the way, his legs stop at his knees and his arms stop at the elbows. Kyle Maynard was born with congenital amputation, which is the absence of a fetal limb or fetal parts at birth. One in two thousand babies is born with all or part of a limb missing, ranging from part of a finger to the absence of both arms and both legs.

Many other people might have given up. Not Kyle. His family would not let him. His father reportedly told his mother that if Kyle could not feed himself, he would starve to death.

There would be no excuses in the Maynard home. That was simply the way it was, and it was the title of Kyle's book that was published in 2005. His philosophy was, "It is not what I can do; it is what I WILL do."

What has Kyle Maynard done with the rest of his life? He lives in a three-story home, can type fifty words per minute, and is able to drive a vehicle. He left college and began a speaking career that has taken him to five continents. Along the way, he made the time to climb a little mountain in Africa. Maynard hiked and crawled his way to the top of the 19,340-foot Mt. Kilimanjaro.

Why? To send a message, especially to people with disabilities, that you can succeed against your obstacles. Kyle Maynard is just one example of someone who has overcome incredible challenges. I would encourage you to read about a few others. You can read the inspiring story about Maynard's life on his website www.kyle-maynard.com.

Nick Vujicic is an Australian evangelist and motivational speaker, who was born with tetra-amelia syndrome, a rare disorder characterized by the absence of all four limbs. You can read more about Nick at lifewithoutlimbs.org.

Sean Stephenson was born with osteogenesis imperfecta, a genetic disorder more commonly known as brittle bone disease. He had more than two hundred fractures during the first thirty-three years of his life. He is three feet tall and confined to a wheelchair. He, too, is a speaker. He earns up to $30,000 per speaking engagement. In every speech, Stephenson challenges his audiences to stop making excuses and take control of their lives. "Get off your 'but,'" he says. That is not a typographical mistake. Stephenson means that we should stop making excuses, such as, "but this" or "but that."

Bethany Hamilton was surfing on October 31, 2003. There was nothing unusual about that. It was what she did. Her life changed that day when a fourteen-foot tiger shark severed her left arm in the waters off Hawaii. She lost 60 percent of her blood after the attack. The lifeguards on duty that day and her doctors said her faith saved her life.

This teenager did not just survive a horrible attack. She was surfing again one month later, and in 2007, she turned pro. A movie was made about her life. I read an article about Hamilton prior to the release of *Soul Surfer*. We can learn much from her zeal for life. Here are her four strategies for success.

1. Focus on what is important.
2. Face your fears.
3. Push yourself to do what you think you cannot do.
4. Be joyful.

Read more about Bethany Hamilton at bethanyhamilton.com.

Jim Abbott reached the major leagues and pitched for the New York Yankees and three other teams. The left-handed pitcher—it was his only hand—threw a no-hitter during his major-league career.

Abbott was asked about his advice to children with disabilities. "Never allow the circumstances of your life to become an excuse. People will allow you to do it. But I believe we have a personal obligation to make the most of the abilities we have. The focus has to remain on what has been given, not what has been taken away. It is the only choice" (Abbott). Read more about Jim Abbott at jimabbott.net.

As I read about each of these individuals, I thought back to my then sixteen-month-old daughter and her congenital heart defect. We decided that day that we too would live with no excuses. If we had made excuses for Kyle, she would never have learned to read, she would not be doing volunteer work, it is unlikely she would be helping two different teachers in their classrooms in two different schools, and she most certainly would not have gone to Haiti on a mission trip.

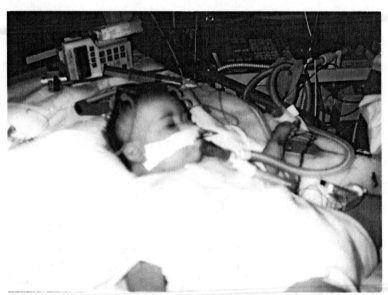

This is a few days after surgery that gave Kyle a longer and better quality life.
I am reminded every time I look at it of how thankful I am for the gift of life.

I think she called traveling, which I did a lot of as a basketball official.
It was always good to get home to my family.

Each year, the players and coaches of the University of Kansas men's basketball team host a clinic for Special Olympics. Kyle was able to grab a photo with former center, Jeff Withey.

Kyle and her Special Olympics teammates. It was a pleasant surprise to see their pictures on the side of a van, which was being used by the Kansas Special Olympics to tour the state.

First day of school at age three.

Kyle got to spend some time with these students while she was in Haiti.

Kyle's rookie card photo

A special friend from #1 Hope Street orphanage.

Kyle and her friend Paige. Kyle loves her like a sister.

Hanging out with Mom at Young Life camp.

Go for the gold.

Our family

Kyle had an extraordinary relationship with her grandfathers, both of whom passed away within a seven-month period. Here are letters written by Kyle, which were read at their respective funerals. Although Kyle has good penmanship, they have been typed for easier reading.

Grandpa Larsen —
From your granddaughter Kyle

Dear Grandpa,

I always love you. You are so special to me. You were a great coach for golf and swimming and basketball and volleyball. Thank you for helping me. You were so proud of me. Thank you for coming to my basketball games for school and Special Olympics.

I liked coming to your house to spend the night and I liked going out to eat with you and grandma. Thank you for protecting our country at the USA Force. We are sad that you are gone. You are in a perfect place. Thank you for being my grandpa. I always love you and place your life in my heart and into my world. I will be good for my mom and daddy for you. I didn't know you were going. I forgot to say good bye. It is you I really love. I liked to mess up your hair.

We all love you very much. Your loving granddaughter Kyle.

Grandpa Martin

Grandpa I love you. I really miss you. You took me and Ernie and Andy to happy hour at the Sonic where everything is half price. Thank you for breakfast at True Lies. Did you like going to Dollywood with us and to family camp. You are the best grandpa. Thank you for going to church with me and for being my Sunday school teacher. And thank you for letting me sing in the Celebration of Freedom choir with you.

Thank you for giving to the Lord I am a life that has changed.

For God so loved the world that he gave his only son that who so ever believes in Him should not perish but have eternal life.

Chapter 8

Hope

"There are seldom, if ever, any hopeless situations, but there are many people who lose hope in the face of some situations" (Ziglar, 1990). In his book, *Up, Down, or Sideways*, Mark Sanborn wrote, "The greatest bankruptcy you will face is not about finances; it is a loss of hope" (Sanborn, 2011, 161).

We experienced a few bleak days after Kyle was born, but we never lost hope. Every small step, every small victory in her life, provided us with a little more hope. While watching and waiting for her to learn to talk and walk, we grabbed every positive sign, like the day she began moving her hands as the song "The Itsy Bitsy Spider" played on her recorder. Not ironically, that is one of the songs we played for her in the days following her heart surgery.

Seeing God heal her and save her life right before our eyes only fueled our hope. Getting through those long, difficult days gave us the strength and courage to survive most anything.

Gene Chizik is the former head football coach at Auburn University. His team was undefeated and won the Bowl Championship Series in 2011. Prior to that they had two miserable seasons during which his teams won only five games.

Chizik wrote a book titled *ALL IN: What It Takes to Be the Best* after winning the national title. The book is a message of hope and encouragement. The coach was interviewed after the book was released and asked about his and his team's success. The interviewer asked him how he was able to lead Auburn to a national championship in his first season after compiling a record of 5 and 19 in the two previous seasons at Iowa State. Five wins in two seasons—sometimes five wins in one season—can cost a college football coach his job. Gene said he just persevered, worked through his trials, and never lost hope. "Everyone has their 5 and 19," he said (Chizik, 2012). We can learn from Gene Chizik.

A few of the 5 and 19s our family experienced include the fact that Kyle often processes information a little slower. And because of her vision, she still needs assistance—another pair of eyes—when she crosses the street. The future is uncertain for all of us. Kyle's Down syndrome and related physical issues adds to her uncertainty and level of independence.

Kyle faced another 5 and 19 when she lost both of her grandfathers within six months of one another. Death is part of the cycle of life, but it was a challenge to explain to Kyle.

What is your 5 and 19? Are you living it now? Stay close to the people who know you best and can walk beside you. Don't lose hope. Don't ever lose hope.

Chapter 9

Expectations

Perhaps one of the best things we did for Kyle was to hire a reading tutor. Today, Kyle loves to read, and she reads well. She also spells rather well. In fact, she amazes me. She can spell words aloud better than she can write them on paper.

One summer evening, we took refuge in a friend's—the Slaytons—basement after a tornado warning was issued. We were all visiting when someone's name was mentioned. I asked Kerri and Judy, "Is she (the woman we were talking about) d-a-n-g-e-r-o-u-s?" Kyle was within earshot and immediately said, "Dangerous." The ladies looked at each other with their eyes and mouths wide open. I made a mental note about spelling out loud. I thought, *The girl is good.*

One day Kyle changed the lyrics to a popular children's song, "This Little Light of Mine." Kids usually learn this song in church. Kyle was singing it one day, a little differently than I remembered it. One sentence is supposed to be, "Don't let Satan blow it out, I'm gonna let it shine." That day, it became, "Don't let *Slayton* blow it out."

Her learning to read brought an added bonus. It helped prepare her to serve. We never dreamed that Kyle would one day return to the elementary school as a volunteer mentor in the classroom. She was given an opportunity to work three mornings a week assisting in the kindergarten classroom. As we helped Kyle prepare for this new adventure, we did not know exactly how she would handle the mentoring or where it would lead. We have been pleasantly surprised.

The following paragraphs are the thoughts of Amie Oltman, a kindergarten teacher who asked if Kyle could volunteer in her classroom:

I first met Kyle when she was helping with summer school. I loved the way she was warm and hugging every one of the students that came in the classroom. I thought to myself that my kindergarten students would sure benefit from a warm hug each and every day. So when I asked for Kyle's phone number to discuss this idea with Kyle's mother, my only expectations for her would be a greeter. I was envisioning in my head that Kyle could be like the Wal-Mart greeter of kindergarten. Never in a million years would I have dreamed Kyle was capable of doing so much in my classroom.

In one of my favorite childhood movies, Pollyanna quotes Abraham Lincoln by saying, "If you look for the bad in people expecting to find it, you surely will." I feel guilty about saying this, but when I first met Kyle, I was not expecting much. I thought she could sharpen a few pencils, but she would probably have to do it in my room because she would need some help or supervision. Clearly, I was mistaken. Yes, she has Down syndrome, but she can do more than I ever expected. I do not have to tell her every day what her responsibilities are. She merely does her job and asks me if there is anything else.

She does the opposite of what I thought she would do when she came into my room.

I remember listening to her while she was practicing naming letters and the letter sounds. She looked at one of our students and said, "I have Down syndrome and I can read. You need to pay attention and try." Since then, this little boy has tried extremely hard for Kyle and me.

One of the major ideas I would stress is if you have a special-needs student, please do not limit your expectations like I did. Look inside for the good in people, and you will find it. I promise!

As Kyle's father, I also had the opportunity to reflect on Kyle's mentoring experience with the kindergarten students. I could not help but think of when she was that age. I thought about all of her years in school.

During the early years of her life when we were learning everything we could about being parents to a child with Down syndrome, we would hear stories about the struggles many parents faced when it came to educating their children. We were urged to stand in the gap and fight tirelessly on Kyle's behalf. We had only a few struggles. There were a few "professionals" who were abrupt at best and maybe even a bit mean spirited. It seemed to be more apparent during mandated Individual Education Plan (IEP) meetings. I suppose if I had to attend several of those meetings, my patience could wear a little thin. But these were professionals, and I expected more from them.

On the days when they were curt, Kerri would leave the meetings in tears. It was frustrating and painful to hear how far behind her peers Kyle was—academically, emotionally, and physically. We knew that, and we did not want to continually be reminded of it.

One principal went the extra mile for Kyle. In one of those IEP meetings, he took Kyle's cell phone and put his number in it with instructions for her to call him if she needed anything.

Our family's approach was to be proactive. We knew Kyle's teachers, and they knew our family. We told them on the first day of school to expect her to follow directions. We did not want her Down syndrome to be an excuse for misbehaving.

Now that Kyle is older, she not only mentors in the kindergarten classroom, but she also works one day a week at the local senior center. The former director of the center, Diane Solorio, is a family friend who taught Kyle to swim. They have had a strong bond since the day Kyle was born.

I often forget that Kyle has Down syndrome. To me, she is just a funny, beautiful, talented, spirited young lady. Not long after she was born, I came to see Kyle. I was very pregnant with Abi, and after your birthing trauma, which of course I knew about, I was scared this could happen to us. We chose not to have the prenatal testing for disability issues because to us, the testing was a nonissue. I wanted, and in some ways needed, to see Kyle. The very interesting thing was that I fell in love with her just like I would any other baby. I knew then that if this was our fate, we would be okay. I understand that in no way, shape, or form, do I know how difficult your parenting life has been. But I do know that because of our visit when she was so tiny, I knew I could love a disabled child. Love comes so easily to Kyle.

My first true adventure with Kyle was caring for her in our house. My goal was not to treat her any differently than I would any other child in my care. Really, I believe the other kids did not know she was different. She got around on all fours as fast as they ran; she talked to me and told me what she wanted; and she played with the other kids. We loved her as our own.

I don't remember swimming being an issue. She was a bit more scared than some, and she was more comfortable than others I have taught.

Kyle and the T-ball team is another story in itself. My husband, John, LOVED her on his team. John has a hand that does not function as a normal hand, so he understands what it feels like to struggle with things that others find so easy. We were honored that you would trust your precious girl to us on the ball field. The other girls just knew Kyle would play, no questions asked. John always talked to the opposing coach about Kyle and made sure the other team understood that she would play, and she would get to run the bases. That was a big thing for John. It helped him grow as a man and also made him thankful for our children and their abilities.

Your daughter showed me early in her life that I could love any child of God's. I thought I could, but holding her and seeing her beautiful eyes, I felt a peace about the child I had not yet delivered. I have been blessed through the years in many ways to be a part of Kyle's life. Has she touched me? Of course! Do I find her challenging? Not really. When you love someone, you simply work through the hard moments to get to the easy ones. The bottom line is I love your daughter. And so do my husband and kids.

Chapter 10

Faith

I do not know how people navigate this life without faith in God. I simply could not have made it.

Every day of Kyle's life, I have lived with a deep and lasting peace that I cannot explain. It is not a peace that was brought about by the absence of conflict. It is a peace that allowed our family to face Down syndrome and a heart defect squarely in the face with much confidence.

Jesus said, "Peace I leave with you; my peace I give you. I do not give to you as the world gives. Do not let your heart be troubled and do not be afraid" (John 14:27).

I remember our pastor coming to the hospital in the middle of the night after Kyle was born. I also remember him sharing a verse of scripture that came to him as he drove to the hospital. "Trust in the Lord with all your heart and lean not on your own understanding; in all your ways acknowledge him and he will make your paths straight" (Proverbs 3:5–6).

I always try to read further, at least one or two verses. In this case, I read verse 7, which tells us not to be wise in our own eyes. The birth of a child with Down syndrome was no time to think that I had everything under control and that I knew what to do and how and when to do it. The truth is, no matter how wise I might have thought I was, I did not have things under control. Not even close. I wanted to be strong, but I was weak and clueless.

Many other verses spoke to me during the first few days of Kyle's life. A defining moment for me came when I read John 9:1–3, the passage where Jesus healed the man who was born blind. "As he went along, he saw a man blind from birth. His disciples asked him, 'Rabbi, who sinned, this man or his parents, that he was born blind?' 'Neither this man nor his parents sinned,' said Jesus, 'but this happened so that the work of God might be displayed in his life.'" Christ used this man's suffering to teach about faith and glorifying God. I believe He used Down syndrome to teach me that and make me stronger.

That verse also comforted me. I was able to visit with a geneticist a few days after Kyle was born. When he assured me that Kyle's Down syndrome was not the result of anything we did or did not do, I was fine. It was as if verse 3 confirmed that none of us did anything wrong. We have been given a daughter with Down syndrome so that the work of God might be displayed in her life.

Sometimes it is hard, or even impossible, to understand why things happen like they do. You just have to trust. The words from Ecclesiastes 11:5 seemingly leaped off the page one day not long after she was born. "As you do not know the path of the wind, or how the body is formed inside a mother's womb, so you cannot understand the work of God, the Maker of all things." I did not understand it at first, but I trusted. And I am still trusting today.

Do not be alarmed when you have trials and troubles. The apostle Paul warned Timothy that he would face trouble, and when he did, he should endure hardship. We can keep going through our suffering because we have hope. Hope is not a wish, but rather it is an unshakeable confidence in the future. When adversity happens, don't freak out.

"Sometimes God calms the storm. At other times, He calms the sailor. And sometimes, He makes us swim."—Anonymous

One of my favorite songs, "It Is Well with My Soul"[1] took on new meaning after Kyle was born. Horatio Spafford wrote it during a storm in his life.

"When peace, like a river, attendeth my way,
When sorrows like sea billows roll;
Whatever my lot, Thou hast taught me to say,
It is well, it is well with my soul."

Faith is what helped me when I had these feelings and thoughts:

- This is the hardest thing I have ever had to deal with.
- Down syndrome and heart surgery are some of the most painful words I have ever heard.
- Becoming a parent on these terms is my biggest fear.
- This is the most uncertainty I have ever faced.
- I am too scared to worry, and too numb to cry.
- I feel guilty and like a failure, but I have to be strong.

---

[1] "It Is Well with My Soul," hymn written by Horatio G. Spafford, 1873. Public domain.

Chapter 11

Changing Seasons

When Kyle became a teenager, the gap between her and her peers began to widen, and it widened significantly. When her friends turned sixteen, most of them started driving. Kyle did not. She will never be able to drive. Even if she had been mentally able to operate a motor vehicle, her low vision would have made it difficult to pass that part of the driver's test.

It is not as if Kyle has been denied many of the same opportunities some of her friends enjoyed. Far from it. In fact, her camping experiences might have been as good, if not better, than many of her friends.

Heather's Camp, a camp for visually impaired young people, is unique. Campers have the opportunity to go horseback riding, canoeing, swimming, and more. Heather's Camp honors the memory of Heather Muller, her love of children, and her desire to help those with special needs. It provides an opportunity for blind and visually impaired children to experience the joy of a camp program where they can acquire skills, gain confidence, find support and encouragement, and have fun.

Kyle also had the opportunity to attend Young Life camps. Young Life is a mission devoted to introducing adolescents to Jesus Christ and helping them grow in their faith. Young Life reaches out to all middle and high-school students, including young people with disabilities. Young Life Capernaum allows kids with disabilities to fully participate in activities that build self-esteem, challenge their limits, and help them discover their ability to do new things.

At times, it was difficult to watch her try to fit in—wanting to fit in, but being unable to. It was painful to see kids ignore her and hide from her. Kyle would think they were playing, but most of the time they were not. None of that bothered Kyle because she loved unconditionally in ways that are unnatural for many of us.

One particular day, as we left church, we walked by a room that was being made ready for a birthday party. The party was for a peer in Kyle's Sunday school class. Kyle saw boxes of pizza and asked the hostess whose it was. The mom replied that is was for her daughter's birthday. If that bothered Kyle, she never showed it. She never gave it another thought. My wife, however, felt the sting of rejection for Kyle. She said, "That probably did not affect others, but it had a profound effect on me, especially when I walked by the room and it was full of Kyle's sixteen-year-old peers."

We do not know of anyone who intentionally went out of his or her way to be insensitive. It is understandable that some might have been uncomfortable around someone like Kyle, perhaps not knowing what to say or do. For too many years, I used to be one of them.

One government official put her ignorance and arrogance on display for all to see. In fact, it went beyond ignorance and arrogance. It bordered on bigotry. Former Surgeon General Joycelyn Elders testified before the Senate Labor Committee on the Freedom of Choice Act during the early 1990s. She said that abortion had a "positive public health effect" because it decreased the number of children afflicted with birth defects. She quoted a statistic that explained that the number of Down syndrome infants in one state was down 64 percent and would have been higher without legalized abortion.[*]

---

[*] As stated by US Senator Don Nickles (R) Oklahoma in a press release on July 2, 1993 regarding a Joycelyn Elders' statement. This statement also appeared in *The Wichita Eagle* on July 31, 1993 (byline was from *Los Angeles Times/Washington Post* service). Don Nickles' response to Ms. Elders' statement can also be reviewed in the Congressional Record, Volume 140, Issue 36, March 25, 1994, http://www.gpo.gov/fdsys/pkg/CREC-1994-03-25/html/CREC-1994-03-25-pt1-PgH9.htm.

Chapter 12

The R Word

Someone told us shortly after Kyle was born that they sympathized with us. We were not looking for sympathy, not in the least. We wanted people to rejoice with us. What we have experienced as a family is not nearly as challenging as what many other families face. We have been blessed to have many family members and friends stand beside and support us during the more difficult days. Sadly, many families do not have that.

Do you want to make a difference in someone's life? Reach out to a family with a special-needs child. You cannot imagine how uplifting that would be and what it would mean to them if you decided to carry their mat directly to Christ, like those four men in Mark's gospel. Your acts of kindness will not be forgotten. I am reminded of something else Zig Ziglar once said: "You never know when a moment and a few sincere words will have an impact on a life" (Ziglar).

Life is fragile. It is fragile for everyone, not just families with special-needs children. So be intentional about connecting with a family. A short, simple note, like one Kerri received shortly after Kyle was born, can be very uplifting.

Kerri,

I just wanted Kyle and you to know that because of her a lot of my ideas about special children have changed. Maybe I have grown up a bit more thanks to Kyle. I will continue to pray for Kyle and all of you.

God Bless!
Sue

I am reminded of an article by Maria Lin, editor-in-chief of *LearnVest* and mother of a boy with special needs. Her article was entitled "7 Things You Don't Know About a Special Needs Parent" (Lin, 2012).

1. I am tired.
2. I am jealous.
3. I feel alone.
4. I am scared.
5. I wish you would stop saying "retarded," or "short bus," or "as long as it is healthy."
6. I am human.
7. I want to talk about my child; it is hard to talk about my child.

Those are Ms. Lin's feelings, but I can relate to each one. A child with special needs makes parenting even more challenging. Let's talk about #5.

In April 2007, some individuals began a campaign to encourage people everywhere to stop using the R word. It was an effort to end the word (retard or retarded), which is a word a newspaper writer said, "is tossed around as a synonym for stupid." The group believes, as do countless others, that it is not about a word; it is about respect.

I have never heard anyone call Kyle retarded, but Kerri has. I do hear the word used in general almost daily. I wrote about it one day in my blog.

I walked into a business this morning. There were three middle-aged men visiting. I don't know who they were or what they had been talking about, but the first words I heard when I entered were, "They are just so retarded."

I closed the door and walked to wait in line. The man who was talking to the others when I walked in looked in my direction and said something about how they were just talking about how some people are just so retarded. I said, "Oh, I don't know. I live with one who is pretty special. In fact, she has made me a much better person." It was not but a few seconds until the topic of their conversation changed.

I wish they knew my daughter. I think she is pretty special. She is sensitive to others, loves everyone, will never forget a thing about you, and can hold her own in a spelling bee. I have said before, and I wish I had told that group of men, that we all should have Down syndrome for a few days. The world would be a better place; I am sure of it. If we all had Down syndrome, there would be unconditional love and forgiveness, and everyone would get a minimum of three hugs per day.

I am not angry with those men, not at all. I just wish they knew someone like my daughter. If Kyle had been with me that morning, she would have shaken every hand in the room; asked about their families and children; asked what they had for dinner the night before; and given them a high five. That is who she is. She does not see skin color, developmental delays, or any other differences many of us see.

Today, only 10 percent of churches have a ministry to individuals with special needs or just considering it. You can begin to make a case that if churches began to minister to families with special-needs children, the divorce rate would begin to decline. Kyle's speech therapist, Jane, felt strongly about the divorce rate among couples with special-needs children. She wanted to make sure we were not a statistic.

The slow pace of progress, paired with the demands of extra time required to take the child to doctor and therapy visits, and the therapy itself, is very draining emotionally and financially. Some parents become so devoted to their child that they leave no time for themselves or each other. It is difficult to juggle, and the feelings of guilt, anger, and frustration interfere with their relationships. Parenting is rewarding but also time consuming and exhausting, and even more so when the child has special needs.

I am reminded of two life lessons. Glenn Jones, Kyle's Special Olympics head coach, says his life lesson is patience. You can never have too much patience. The other lesson is from my wife. It is a reminder to treat people with special needs and their families with the same respect we want Kyle to receive.

Chapter 13

Words to Live By

I spend a fair amount of time most evenings playing the electronic version of *Scrabble*. When I think of words, I am reminded of Duke's head basketball coach, Mike Krzyzewski, the winningest college basketball coach in America. He wrote a book many years ago entitled *Beyond Basketball*. In the book, he takes powerful words, forty-seven of them in all, and creates an entire chapter for each word. Krzyzewski encourages the reader not to use or borrow the words but to own them. That prompted me to think of a few words to share with you. Don't just use or borrow them; own them. Make them your own. Here is my list:

ADVERSITY—Adversity is inevitable. It is also invaluable and can make you stronger than you ever imagined.

BOLD—Live boldly. You are going to leave a legacy, so let it be bold.

COUNSEL—Do not be the least bit afraid to seek counsel from wise people. There is nothing weak about that.

EXCELLENCE—Strive for excellence. You are not perfect and never will be perfect, but you should still strive for excellence.

FAITH—I like how Max Lucado said it: "Faith is trusting what the eye can't see" (Lucado, 1999). For me, that included trusting that God would give me the strength and courage to be a good dad to a daughter with special needs. Twenty-three years ago, I would have told you I was not sure how I was going to get through this parenting thing. It took giving me a daughter with Down syndrome to mold me into the person I am today.

FAILURE—John Maxwell, America's authority on leadership, said we need to learn to fail forward. Failure does not have to be fatal or final. Maxwell tells the story of leadership expert Warren Bennis, who interviewed dozens of the nation's top performers. Bennis found that none of them viewed their mistakes as failures. Instead, they looked at them as opportunities for growth. We should too.

FAMILY—Like my faith, I do not know where I would be without my family. You are rich if you are part of a family (including a church family) that loves you.

FRIENDS—If you do not have a friend who you can call at three o'clock in the morning, you do not have deep enough friendships.

GIVE—Be a giver. Bob Burg has a great book I would encourage you to read. It is entitled *Go Giver*. Give back something.

HOPE—NEVER lose hope.

INTEGRITY—Lose this and you lose.

LOVE—Love life. Love the people in your life.

MONEY—You had better know how to manage it. Do not let it manage you.

PATIENCE—You are going to need a good supply of this. My problem is that I want it right now.

READ—If people cannot read and learn to manage their resources, their options in life will be limited. I believe there is a correlation between illiteracy and trials in life. The trials will seemingly never end. That is why I am devoting the rest of my life to the fight against illiteracy. Read and encourage others, especially children.

RELATIONSHIPS—Life is all about relationships. Invest in making yours stronger.

Chapter 14

God Knows Your Name

I began writing this book during basketball season. March, the busiest time of the season, is when all of the season-ending tournaments happen. There is a reason it is known as March Madness. It is usually exciting and even a little wacky.

College basketball in particular receives much television exposure. It culminates with the Final Four, which, in my opinion, is one of the greatest events in sports. Fans are knowledgeable and understand the game. They know the players' names in addition to many other personal things about them.

There is another tournament every March. It is played in smaller arenas throughout the United States and is played by athletes whose skill level is nowhere near as good as the college athletes who play in the Final Four. I am referring to the Special Olympics.

It occurred to me as I watched my daughter participate in the state tournament where, aside from family members and a few friends, people do not know the names of these special athletes. But God does. He not only knows their names, but He also knows about them personally, their families, and the struggles they face.

God also knows you and me, and He has a plan for each one of us. He even knows the number of hairs on our heads. He loves us, and no matter what happens, you can take comfort in knowing that.

Afterword

Jan Thompson is a family friend and missionary serving in Haiti. Not long after Jan arrived in Haiti, she started an orphanage.

Once when Jan was home on furlough, she spoke at our church about her ministry. Kyle was there that night. Following the service, our pastor encouraged people to consider going to Haiti on a mission trip, specifically to Christopher's Hope, the orphanage our friend had started. He had barely said amen before Kyle met the pastor at the pulpit asking, "Pastor, when does the bus leave?" We all thought it was cute and we laughed. Kyle and God were not laughing. They were serious.

Several teams from our church made trips to Haiti, including Kyle's grandmother. She has been there eight times. She was able to take all five of her daughters in 1975 and dreamed of accompanying Kyle.

Kyle continued to talk about going to Haiti to help serve God, Jan, and the "Hopesters" at the orphanage. I had my doubts about whether it would be possible. My doubts were:

"She has Down syndrome."

"Haiti is the poorest place on the face of the earth."

"It is filthy in Haiti. Will she keep her dirty hands away from her mouth?"

Oh ye of little faith.

Kerri had been on three previous mission trips to the country. We decided if Kyle wanted to go, we should do what we could to make it happen.

In November 2013, three years after she first learned of an orphanage in Haiti, Kyle went. She even met another little girl with Down syndrome. She helped in a classroom teaching the six- and seven-year-old students to read and write in English. She sang with them and monitored recess just as she does in the States.

Jan's thoughts on Kyle's mission trip:

Kyle told everyone she met that she was going to go to Haiti someday, and I knew she would. I had only two concerns about her coming to Haiti. My first concern was that Kyle DOES NOT like dogs, and I had two of them—big ones! So we put the dogs on the roof with a big metal door between them and Kyle. Problem solved.

My second concern was for Kyle's spiritual protection. Many people (including children) come to our ministry and have frightening experiences due to the Satanic/demonic influences in Haiti. Weak faith is a target for the enemy, but on Day #1, Kyle showed this was not going to be a problem for her. She met a new staff member, found out her name, and then said, "Do you know God?" Her boldness let Satan know that she was in Haiti as a soldier for her King. I think he figured out he was no match for the zeal of Kyle Loucks!

I was so bountifully blessed to watch her tenderly hug the Hopesters, tell them they were beautiful, teach them songs, laugh with them, play with them, and pray with them. She never wanted to slow down even long enough to sleep; she wanted to experience it all. She brought a renewed passion to my work with the Hopesters. Seeing them through her eyes reminded me to enjoy every minute I have with them.

Kyle Loucks, I love you so much, and I will never forget your first trip to Haiti. You blessed me, girlfriend! I look forward to you returning to Haiti.

Jan Thompson
Christopher's Hope Ministry
Gonaives, Haiti

"For nothing is impossible with God" (Luke 1:37).

Thirty-eight years after the first family trip, three generations were serving together again in Haiti. Kyle's grandmother was overjoyed to get to experience the trip with Kyle.

Kyle is ready to go again. I asked her why. She replied, "To serve the kids and God."

References

Abbott, Jim. FAQ: Overcoming Adversity. Advice to Parents and Children with Challenges. http://www.jimabbott25.com/ abbottfaq_ overcoming.html

Chizik, Gene. *ALL IN: What It Takes to Be the Best.* 2012. Illinois: Tyndale House Publishers.

Gordon, Jon. 20 Tips for a Positive New Year. http://www. jongordon.com/positive-tip-new-year-2013.html

Gorham, Dick. *It's Just Life: A Small Story Within a Greater Story.* 2009. Newton, KS: Mennonite Press, Inc.

Lin, Maria, 2012. "7 Things You Don't Know About a Special Needs Parent." *Huffington Post,* March 9. www.huffingtonpost. com/maria-lin/special-needs-parenting_b_1314348.html

Lucado, Max. *When God Whispers Your Name.* 1999. Nashville, TN: Thomas Nelson.

Maxwell, Jon. *The 15 Invaluable Laws of Growth.* 2012. New York: Center Street.

Sanborn, Mark. *Up, Down, or Sideways.* 2011. Illinois: Tyndale House Publishers.

Shook, Kerry and Chris. *One Month to Live*. 2008. New York: WaterBrook Press.

ThinkExist. James Arthur Baldwin quotes. http://thinkexist.com/quotation/not_everything_that_is_faced_can_be_changed-but/7880.html

Ziglar, Zig. *The Little Book of Big Quotes*. 1990. Zig Ziglar.

Ziglar, Zig. Search "You never know when a moment . . ." www.ziglar.com.

CPSIA information can be obtained at www.ICGtesting.com
Printed in the USA
BVOW03s1213180214

345264BV00008B/108/P

9 781613 141946